Giant Beaver

by Julie Murray

Abdo
ICE AGE ANIMALS
Kids

Abdo Kids Jumbo is an Imprint of Abdo Kids
abdobooks.com

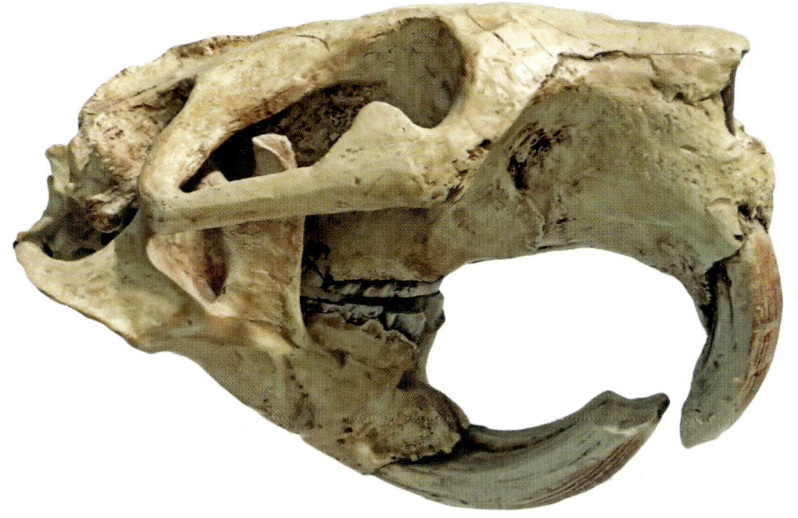

abdobooks.com

Published by Abdo Kids, a division of ABDO, P.O. Box 398166, Minneapolis, Minnesota 55439. Copyright © 2024 by Abdo Consulting Group, Inc. International copyrights reserved in all countries. No part of this book may be reproduced in any form without written permission from the publisher. Abdo Kids Jumbo™ is a trademark and logo of Abdo Kids.

Printed in the United States of America, North Mankato, Minnesota.

052023
092023

 THIS BOOK CONTAINS RECYCLED MATERIALS

Photo Credits: Alamy, Science Source, Shutterstock, Studio 252MYA, ©James St. John p.1,15 / CC BY 2.0, ©Jimmy Emerson, DVM p.9 / CC BY-NC-ND 2.0, ©Roman Uchyte p.11,15, ©Blue Rhino Studio p.13

Production Contributors: Teddy Borth, Jennie Forsberg, Grace Hansen
Design Contributors: Candice Keimig, Pakou Moua

Library of Congress Control Number: 2022946797

Publisher's Cataloging-in-Publication Data

Names: Murray, Julie, author.
Title: Giant beaver / by Julie Murray
Description: Minneapolis, Minnesota : Abdo Kids, 2024 | Series: Ice age animals | Includes online resources and index.
Identifiers: ISBN 9781098266349 (lib. bdg.) | ISBN 9781098267049 (ebook) | ISBN 9781098267391 (Read-to-me ebook)
Subjects: LCSH: Animals--Juvenile literature. | Extinct animals--Juvenile literature. | Ice Age--Juvenile literature. | Paleontology--Juvenile literature. | Zoology--Juvenile literature.
Classification: DDC 569--dc23

Table of Contents

Ice Age 4

Giant Beaver 6

Food 18

Extinction 20

More Facts 22

Glossary 23

Index 24

Abdo Kids Code 24

Ice Age

An ice age is a period when most of the Earth is covered in sheets of ice. The last ice age began about 100,000 years ago. It lasted until about 12,000 years ago. Some animals became **extinct** during this time in history.

Giant Beaver

The giant beaver appeared around 1.4 million years ago. It was only found in North America. It lived in wetlands. It swam in lakes, swamps, and ponds.

The giant beaver was the largest rodent to ever live in North America. It was the size of a black bear!

It was 7 feet (2.1 m) long and stood 3 feet (0.91 m) tall. It could weigh up to 225 pounds (102 kg)!

11

The giant beaver was covered in shaggy, brown fur. Its tail was long and thin. It had large, **webbed** back feet. These made it an excellent swimmer.

13

It had giant **incisor** teeth that grew 6 inches (15 cm) long. The teeth were thick and curved.

15

Scientists believe that the giant beaver did not use its teeth to chew on wood. They also do not think that it built dams like modern beavers.

Food

The giant beaver ate **aquatic** plants. It liked leaves, roots, and cattails.

Extinction

The giant beaver became **extinct** about 12,000 years ago. It is believed that the loss of its habitat was the main cause. This was due to the warming temperatures.

More Facts

- The first giant beaver **fossils** were discovered in 1837 in a **peat bog** in Ohio.

- It is a distant relative to modern beavers. It is more like the modern capybara.

- It spent more time in the water than on land. It had short back legs, which made it difficult to walk on land.

- It had a much smaller brain than modern beavers.

Glossary

aquatic – living or growing in water.

extinct – no longer existing.

fossil – the remains or trace of a living animal or plant from a long time ago.

incisor – in mammals, one of the four sharp teeth located between the canines in each jaw at the front of the mouth.

peat bog – soft, wet ground containing soil made up of dead plants, or peat.

webbed – joined by skin.

Index

climate change 20

color 12

feet 12

food 18

fur 12

habitat 6, 20

range 6

size 8, 10

tail 12

teeth 14, 16

weight 10

Visit **abdokids.com** to access crafts, games, videos, and more!

Use Abdo Kids code **IGK6349** or scan this QR code!